For Sale

By Eve Bunting

Illustrated by Malcolm Stokes

Dominie Press, Inc.

Publisher: Raymond Yuen
Project Editor: John S. F. Graham
Editor: Bob Rowland
Designer: Greg DiGenti
Illustrator: Malcolm Stokes

Published by:

ꝑ Dominie Press, Inc.

1949 Kellogg Avenue
Carlsbad, California 92008 USA

www.dominie.com

1-800-232-4570

Paperback ISBN 0-7685-2061-4
Printed in Singapore by PH Productions Pte Ltd
1 2 3 4 5 6 PH 05 04 03

Table of Contents

Chapter One
We Hate It Already!

"**G**irls! Come sit next to us," Dad said.

Gwen and Lily left their jigsaw puzzle and went across the room to the couch.

"We have something to tell you," Dad said. And then he said to Mom, "You tell them."

Gwen thought that wasn't a good sign. Whenever something was hard to say, Dad liked to pass it along to Mom. What could it be?

Mom gave Dad a look that said, "Thanks a lot." Then she smiled down at Gwen and Lily.

"Well, we've decided to sell our house and buy another one. Isn't that exciting?"

"Sell our house?" Gwen sat straight up on the edge of the couch.

Lily put her thumb in her mouth. She was only five, and she still sucked her thumb sometimes.

"We're going to need a bigger house," Dad said, "now that the baby's coming."

"But babies are little," Gwen protested. "They don't take up that much space." Gwen felt like crying. "We love this house. We don't want to leave!"

"Just think! You girls will each have you own bedroom," Dad said happily.

"But my best friend lives next door," Gwen said.

"And mine lives across the street," Lily said. She had to take her thumb out of her mouth so she could speak.

"We won't move very far," Mom promised. "You'll still be able to see them. You'll make new friends, too. You'll like the new house."

"No, we won't," Lily said.

And Gwen added, "We hate it already!"

Chapter Two
Mouse And All

The next day, a woman from the real estate office came. She walked through the house and made notes. Mom walked around with her. So did Gwen and Lily.

"This is very nice," the woman said when they went into Gwen and Lily's bedroom.

"The paint is flaking off the windowsills," Gwen pointed out.

"And the closet door squeaks," Lily said.

Gwen lowered her voice to a whisper. "One time we had a mouse in our kitchen."

Mom gave them a look. "Stop it, you two!"

The woman laughed. "I guess I know two people who don't want to sell this house," she said. "That's a really good sign. This must be a nice place to live."

Later, she told Mom, "This is a lovely house. I think we can get a very good price for it, mouse and all."

Mom smiled. "I hope so. We can't really buy another house until we find a buyer for this one."

"This will sell quickly, I'm sure," the woman told her. "Tomorrow I will bring over a For Sale sign for the front yard."

Mom walked with her to her car.

Gwen and Lily watched them. Then Gwen said, "Don't worry, Lily. I have lots of ideas."

"You are so smart, Gwen," Lily said.

Chapter Three
It Might Take a While

The next day, the real estate woman brought over the big For Sale sign and stuck it in the front yard.

Gwen's mom and dad stood in front of it, admiring it.

"I bet people will stop for a look when they see this," Dad said.

Then Mom said, "Get your sweaters, girls. We're going to go look at houses to buy today. It may take a while to find something we like."

"We won't like anything," Gwen grumbled. But she went. They all piled into the car and drove up and down lots of streets. They stopped at all the For Sale signs they saw.

"This one's so pretty," Mom said.

"It's yucky," Gwen said.

"Super yucky," Lily said.

At the next house, Gwen said, "Oh! This is the smallest yard I've ever seen. We couldn't even fit our swing set in this yard."

"Way too small," Lily agreed.

"I love this one," Mom said when they stopped at a pink house.

"A *pink* house," Gwen said. "I'd hate

to live in a pink house."

"We could paint it," Dad said. "It could be a family project."

Mom didn't look too sure. "I won't be doing much painting before the baby comes. Not for a while after, either."

Gwen smiled at Lily. Now Mom was finding things wrong with the houses. And later on they saw three more houses that both Mom and Dad didn't like.

"This one needs too much work to make it good to live in," Dad said about one of them.

"This one is too small for a family with three kids," Mom said about another.

When they saw the last house that day, both Mom and Dad looked tired. They both thought it was OK until Gwen pointed out how small the kitchen was and that the fence was falling down.

They went home without having found a house.

"You are so smart," Lily said to her sister. "You can find anything wrong with a house."

The next day they started looking for houses again. Mom and Dad didn't look so eager anymore.

For every house, Gwen pointed out every little fault she could think of. One house didn't have enough electrical outlets, another didn't have a garage door. They saw some that were so far away that Gwen and Lily would have to change schools. Not even Mom and Dad thought that was a good idea.

Gwen was feeling very proud of herself, and Lily didn't have her thumb in her mouth the whole day.

But then, at the end of the day, they saw a perfect house. It had lots of room. It had a big yard. And it had a wide front porch with a rocking chair.

"We could ask if they'd sell the rocker, too," Dad said, and he and Mom smiled at each other.

"It would be a perfect place to sit with the baby," Mom said.

Even Gwen couldn't think of anything to complain about the house. She thought and thought, but there wasn't anything bad about it.

After they saw the whole house, Lily looked up at her sister, worried. Gwen was worried, too. She had to think of something.

"It looks like it's too expensive," she said to her Mom and Dad.

"Not at all," Mom said. "It's just the

right price."

Gwen looked back at Lily, who had put her thumb back in her mouth.

Chapter Four
Another Good Idea

Gwen was worried. They had found a nice house. When they got home, Gwen and Lily went into their room and shut the door.

"Remember when Mom told that real estate woman that they couldn't buy

another house without selling this one
first?" Gwen asked Lily.

Lily nodded.

"We'll just have to keep them from
selling this house," Gwen said.

"What are we going to do?" Lily
asked.

"I have an idea," Gwen said.

"You are so smart," Lily told her.

"I know," Gwen said.

That night, after dinner, Gwen and Lily slipped outside. They took the big For Sale sign and hid it in the bushes. It was heavier than it looked.

First thing in the morning, Dad looked out of the window and said, "Hey! Where's our For Sale sign?"

Gwen and Lily kept on eating their cereal. Dad gave them a suspicious look. He walked outside and found the sign in about two minutes.

"How do you think it got there, girls?" Mom asked.

"Maybe an elephant came in the night and pulled it out," Lily said. "And maybe he carried it behind the bushes in his trunk."

"That's probably what happened," Dad said. He gathered up the two girls in a bear hug. "I know this is hard for you. But your mom and I would never do anything to hurt you. You'll be sad for a day or two when we move. You'll miss your friends. But you'll make new friends. And after that, you'll be OK. I promise."

"And you know what?" Mom added. "Home is home. Any house for us will always be a home as long as we're together."

"Did you buy the other one yet? The one with the big porch and the rocking chair?" Lily asked.

"Not yet," Dad said. "But we plan to put in an offer as soon as we get a nibble on this house."

They didn't have to wait very long. They got a nibble the very next day. In fact, they got a bite.

A woman came. She loved the house. She said she'd come back with her husband that evening at five o'clock.

When she left, Gwen told Lily, "Don't worry. I have another good idea."

"What is it?" Lily asked.

"Wait and see," Gwen said.

Chapter Five

The Pretty House
with the Big Porch

That afternoon, Gwen and Lily went
to their friend Michelle's house and then
across the street to their friend Cathy's
house.

"At five o'clock, I will hang a white
sock out of our bedroom window. That

will be the sign," Gwen told them.
"Then turn on your stereo and your TV loud, loud, loud!"

"My mom will be mad," Michelle said. "She'll just rush and turn them off."

"That's OK. We just need a minute," Gwen said.

"Babette turns up her music, anyway," Cathy told Gwen. "She'll be happy to make it louder." Babette was Cathy's baby-sitter.

"Great!" Gwen said. "Remember the sign."

As soon as the car pulled up outside, at five o'clock exactly, Gwen and Lily ran to hang out the sock.

Music blasted all around them.

"What on Earth?" Mom asked in a puzzled voice.

In just a few minutes, the music

stopped and there was silence again.

"Sometimes we have very noisy neighbors," Gwen told the man and woman who had come to see their house. "You wouldn't like it here."

"Oh, but I would," the man said. "I play the trombone. I try not to be too loud, though."

"I think our girls arranged this," Dad said. "Our neighbors are really very thoughtful."

The man and woman talked together quietly. Then the man said, "We've both fallen in love with your house. We want to buy it."

And they did.

Gwen and Lily tried everything they could think of, but it was no use.

Their parents bought the pretty house with the big porch. At first, Gwen and

Lily were determined not to like it there, but it turned out to be perfect. They each had their own room, and there was a room for the baby. The porch was a great place for summer sleepovers with Michelle and Cathy and their nice new friends, the ten-year-old twins who lived next door.

Gwen and Lily helped paint the

baby's room.

"This is better than painting that whole big pink house," Gwen said.

"I like it a lot here," Lily told her. "Dad and Mom were right. How come parents are right so often?"

"Because they're smart," Gwen said.

"Like you," Lily told her.

"Just like me," Gwen said.